W9-BJM-625

SOUNDS OF LANGUAGE

readers

Holt, Rinehart and Winston, Inc.
New York   Toronto   London   Sydney

SOUNDS AROUND THE CLOCK

BY BILL MARTIN JR.
IN COLLABORATION WITH PEGGY BROGAN

ACKNOWLEDGMENTS

The Author and Holt, Rinehart and Winston, Inc. thank the following authors and publishers, whose help and permissions to reprint materials have made this book possible. All reasonable effort has been made to locate the source of every selection. If any errors in acknowledgments have occurred, they are inadvertent and will be corrected in subsequent editions as they are realized.

The following selections are adapted from Little Owl Books, copyright © 1963 by Holt, Rinehart and Winston, Inc., except as noted.

"All Kinds of Neighbors" from *All Kinds of Neighbors*, by Howard R. Wellesley.

"Baby Elephant" from *Baby Elephant*, by Patricia K. Miller and Iran L. Seligman.

"Big Frogs, Little Frogs" from *Big Frogs, Little Frogs*, by Patricia K. Miller and Iran L. Seligman.

"The House Biter" from *The House Biter*, by William D. Sheldon. Copyright © 1966 by Holt, Rinehart and Winston, Inc.

"The House that Jack Built" from *The House That Jack Built*.

"Round is a Pancake" from *Round is a Pancake*, by Joan Sullivan.

"The Sun Is a Star" from *The Sun Is a Star*, by Sune Engelbrektson.

"This Is My Family" from *This Is My Family*, by Howard F. Fehr.

Other Sources:

Beckley-Cardey Company for "Who Is Tapping at my Window?" by A. G. Deming. Reprinted by permission.

E. P. Dutton & Co., Inc., Methuen & Co., Ltd. and Mr. C. R. Milne, for "The End," from *Now We Are Six*, by A. A. Milne. Copyright 1927 by E. P. Dutton & Co., Inc. Renewal © 1955 by A. A. Milne. Reprinted by permission of the publishers.

Gallay Advertising, Incorporated of Chicago for abstract painting on p. 174, artist unknown.

Copyright © 1972, 1966 by Holt, Rinehart and Winston, Inc. All rights reserved. Printed in the United States of America. Published simultaneously in Canada. Library of Congress Cat. No. 76-154051. Permission must be secured for broadcasting, tape-recording, mechanically duplicating or reproducing in any way any part of this book for any purpose. ISBN: 0-03-083353-1

12345 071 987654321

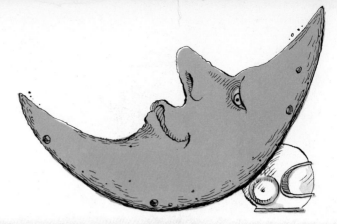

Harcourt Brace Jovanovich, Inc., for "Someday They'll Give a War," a selection from *The People, Yes*, by Carl Sandburg. Copyright 1936 by Harcourt Brace Jovanovich, Inc. Copyright © 1964 by Carl Sandburg. Reprinted by permission of the publisher.

Harcourt Brace Jovanovich, Inc. for "What Did You Put in Your Pocket?" from *Something Special*, by Beatrice Schenk de Regniers, copyright © 1958. Reprinted by permission of Harcourt Brace Jovanovich, Inc. and William Collins Sons.

Highlights for Children, Inc. for "Sun on the Clover," first published as "The Sun," by Louise Fabrice Handcock in *Children's Activities*. Copyright Children's Activities. By permission of Highlights for Children, Inc., Columbus, Ohio.

Little, Brown and Company for "Five Little Monkeys," first published as "The Monkeys and the Crocodile," in *Tirra, Lirra, Rhymes Old and New* by Laura E. Richards. Reprinted by permission.

David McKay Company, Inc. for "Summer Morning," lines from "Summer Morning" in *Christopher O!* by Barbara Young. Copyright 1947 by Barbara Young and reprinted by permission of the publisher.

Rand McNally & Company for "Sally and Manda," from *Sally and Manda* by Alice B. Campbell, from Child Life Magazine. Copyright 1934, © 1962 by Rand McNally & Company.

Charles Scribner's Sons for "So Many Monkeys," from *Open The Door*, by Marion Edey and Dorothy Grider. Copyright 1949 Marion Edey and Dorothy Grider. Reprinted by permission of Charles Scribner's Sons.

The Viking Press, Inc. for "Firefly," from *Under the Tree*, by Elizabeth Madox Roberts. Copyright 1922 by B. W. Huebsch, Inc. Renewed 1950 by Ivor S. Roberts. Reprinted by permission of The Viking Press, Inc.

Joel Weltman for the photograph "Snowy Morning." Reprinted by permission.

Acknowledgment is also made to Betty Jean Martin for permission to use the character, Noodles the Ghost, in this edition of Sounds of Numbers.

And no acknowledgment list would be complete without special thanks and appreciation to Phyllis Stevens and Lydia Vita for their skilled preparation of this book for delivery to the printer.

CONTENTS

This book is dedicated to my friend and colleague
JOHN MILTON PHILLIPS
who has clocked a good many years with me

SOUNDS AROUND THE CLOCK

The End

by A.A. Milne, pictures by Sonia O. Lisker

When I was One,
I had just begun.

When I was Two,
I was nearly new.

15

When I was Three,
I was hardly Me.

When I was Four,
I was not much more.

When I was Five,
I was just alive.

But now I am Six,
    I'm as clever as clever.
So I think I'll be six now
    for ever and ever.

Here's a Picture for Storytelling

by George Buckett

adapted from a story by Joan Sullivan

pictures by Cornelio Martinez

ROUND IS A PANCAKE

Round is a pancake

Round is a plum

Round is a lemon

Round is a lime

Round is a nickel!

Round is a dime

Round is a baseball

Round is a cap

Round is my grandpa

Round is his lap

Round is a puppy
Curled up on a rug

Round are the spots
on a wee lady bug

LOOK ALL AROUND, ON THE GROUND IN THE AIR,
You will find round things EVERYWHERE

Oodles of Noodles

I love noodles. Give me oodles.
Make a mound up to the sun.
Noodles are my favorite foodles.
I eat noodles by the ton.

by Lucia and James L. Hymes, Jr.
picture by George Buckett

So Many Monkeys

Monkey Monkey Moo!
Shall we buy a few?
   Yellow monkeys,
     Purple monkeys,
       Monkeys red and blue.

Be a monkey, do!
Who's a monkey, who?
   He's a monkey,
     She's a monkey,
       You're a monkey, too!

by Marion Edey and Dorothy Grider,
picture by Kelly Oechsli

a story by Mary Ann Lynch,
adapted by Bill Martin Jr.,
with pictures by Muriel Wood

My Name Is Pink
but you can call me Pinkie.

My dress is pink.
My sox are pink.
My ribbons are pink.
And my name is Pink
but you can call me Pinkie.

Now, my dress is red.
My sox are red.
My ribbons are red.
But my name is not Red.
You know what my name is.
My name is Pink
but you can call me Pinkie.

My dress is white.
My gloves are white.
My flowers are white.
My shoes are silver.
And my name is Pink
but you can call me Pinkie.

43

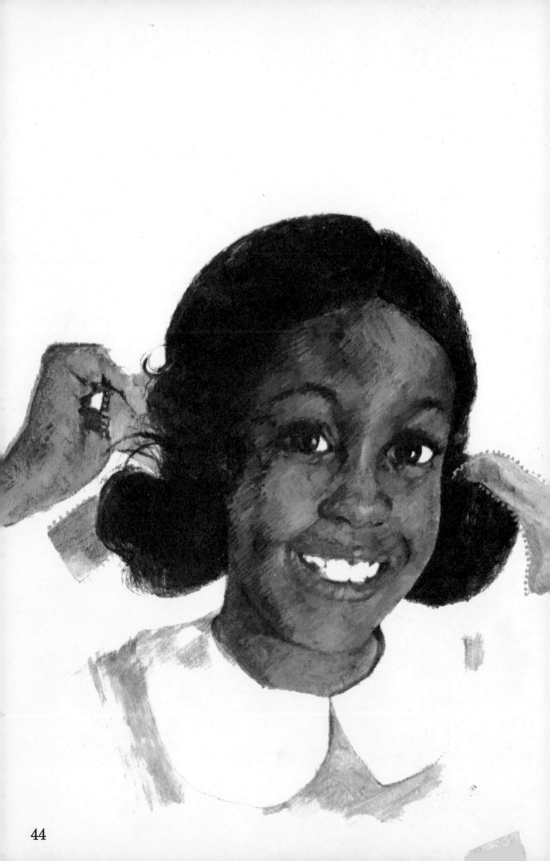

My hair is black
My eyes are brown.
My teeth are white.
My lips are red.
And my name is Pink
but you can call me Pinkie.

Mesa, Ariz - 24 Nov 1925

Here's a Picture for Dreaming

watercolor by LeGreen Richards

Said the kind kangaroo, "Oh, what shall I do? — If I had a cradle, I'd rock it. But my baby is small — so I think — after all, I'll carry her 'round in my pocket."

an old rhyme

48

LOVE is something if you give it away
a traditional song
design by Lynda Barber, lettering by Ray Barber

Baby Elephant

by Patricia K. Miller and Iran L. Seligman,
pictures by Mamoru Funai

This is Ellen.
She is a baby elephant.

She will be a baby
for a long time.
She is three feet tall.
She weighs 200 pounds.

Ellen has small eyes.
She cannot see well.
She has big ears.
She cannot hear well.
Ellen has a long nose.
It is called a trunk.
She uses her trunk in many ways.

When Ellen holds her trunk in the air,
  she can smell things that are far away.
She picks up food.
She pulls up trees.
She pulls down leaves.
She does all this with her trunk.

Ellen has big feet.
She cannot run.
She cannot jump.

But she can walk very fast.

She fills her trunk with water.
She drinks some of the water.
She takes a bath with some of the water.

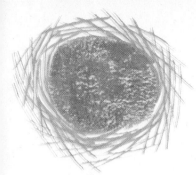

Ellen likes to play.
She slides down a hill.
She plays in the water.
She hides from her mother.

One day Ellen was hiding
  from her mother.
She fell into a deep hole.
She raised her trunk
  and made a **loud** noise.

Mother came to the hole.
When she saw Ellen,
   she raised her trunk
   and made

   a **loud**
        noise.

Other elephants came.
The elephants kicked sand into the hole.

They kicked and kicked.
At last the hole was not so deep.
Ellen climbed out of the hole.

Now Ellen is back with the herd.

Is she looking for another place to hide?

YANKEE DOODLE WENT TO TOWN A-RIDING ON HIS PONY

stuck a feather in his cap

and called it macaroni

There Were Three Ghostesses

Sitting on postesses,
Eating buttered toastesses,
And greasing their fistesses
Right up to the wristesses.
Weren't they beastesses
To make such feastesses!

Three Potatoes in a Pot,

Take one out and leave two hot.
Two potatoes in a pot,
Take one out and leave one hot.
One potato in a pot,
Take it out—
Nothing in the pot.

authors unknown,
pictures by Kelly Oechsli

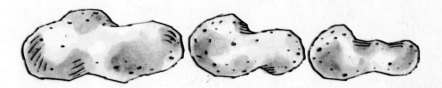

Here's a Picture for Storytelling

by George Buckett

This Is My Family

by Howard F. Fehr,
pictures by Aliki

See!

HAIR-RAISING HIPPO

Hello. My name is Eric.

This is my family.

This is my father.

This is my mother.

This is my brother.

This is my sister.

and this is me.

"Mother, is my dog

a member of our family?"

"Yes, Eric.

Your dog is a member of our family."

Then, this is my family.

Father

Sister   me

Mother   Brother

and my dog.

These are the men in our family.

First, my father. He is a man.

Then my brother.
He is almost a man.

And me.
Someday I will be a man.

These are the women in our family.

First, my mother.
She is a woman.

Then my sister.
She is almost a woman.

Then my dog.
She is a lady dog.

My father is
the oldest member
of our family.
My mother is
next to
the oldest.

Then my brother.
Then my sister.
Then my dog.
Then me.
I am the
   youngest member
   of our family.

"Mother, does my dog have a dog family?"
"Yes, Eric. Your dog has a dog family.

She has a father.

And a mother. And three brothers."

"Mother, am I a member
   of my dog's family?"
"No, Eric. You belong to our family.
   This is our family...

Father,   Mother,

Brother, Sister, your dog, and you."

a song by Woody Guthrie,

drawing by Tom Huffman

88 "This Land Is Your Land," words and music by Woodie Guthrie. TRO—copyright
© 1956 and © 1958 by Ludlow Music, Inc., New York, N.Y. Used by permission.

Here's a Picture for Storytelling

by George Buckett

The House That Jack Built

a tale from Mother Goose
pictures by Donald E. Cooke,
adapted from old drawings by Frederick Richardson

This is the HOUSE that Jack built.

This is the MALT,
That lay in the house
that Jack built.

This is the RAT,
That ate the malt,
That lay in the house
    that Jack built.

This is the CAT,
That killed the rat,
That ate the malt,
That lay in the house
    that Jack built.

This is the DOG,
That worried the cat,
That killed the rat,
That ate the malt,
That lay in the house
   that Jack built.

This is the COW
  with the crumpled horn,
That tossed the dog,
That worried the cat,
That killed the rat,
That ate the malt,
That lay in the house
  that Jack built.

This is the MAIDEN all forlorn,
That milked the cow
  with the crumpled horn,
That tossed the dog,
That worried the cat,
That killed the rat,
That ate the malt,
That lay in the house
  that Jack built.

This is the MAN all tattered and torn,
That kissed the maiden all forlorn,
That milked the cow
   with the crumpled horn,
That tossed the dog,
That worried the cat,
That killed the rat,
That ate the malt,
That lay
   in the house
   that
   Jack
   built.

This is the PRIEST all shaven and shorn,
That married the man all tattered and torn,
That kissed the maiden all forlorn,
That milked the cow
with the crumpled horn,
That tossed the dog,
That worried the cat,
That killed the rat,
That ate the malt,
That lay in the house
that Jack built.

This is the COCK that crowed in the morn,
That waked the priest all shaven and shorn,
That married the man all tattered and torn,
That kissed the maiden all forlorn,
That milked the cow
   with the crumpled horn,
That tossed the dog, that worried the cat,
That killed the rat, that ate the malt,
That lay in the house that Jack built.

This is the FARMER that sowed the corn,

That kept the cock that crowed in the morn,

That waked the priest all shaven and shorn,

That married the man all tattered and torn,

That kissed the maiden all forlorn,

That milked the cow

  with the crumpled horn,

That tossed the dog, that worried the cat,

That killed the rat, that ate the malt,

That lay in the house that Jack built.

Snow snow snow
   Come out! Come out in the snow!
Just look at the snow!
   Come out! Come out in the snow!
Do you like the snow
   Yes or no?
Do you like it in your face?
Yes, I like it any place.

Raphael Conica
AGE 11
photograph by Joel Weltman

Five Little Monkeys

Swinging from a tree;
Teasing Uncle Crocodile,
Merry as can be.
Swinging high, swinging low,
Swinging left and right:
"Dear Uncle Crocodile,
Come and take a bite!"

Four little monkeys
Sitting in a tree;
Heads down, tails down,
Dreary as can be.
Weeping loud, weeping low,
Crying to each other:
"Wicked Uncle Crocodile,
 To gobble up our brother!"

by Laura E. Richards,
picture by Kelly Oechsli

Clouds

White sheep, white sheep,
On a blue hill,
When the wind stops
You all stand still.

When the wind blows
You walk away slow.
White sheep, white sheep,
Where do you go?

by Christina G. Rossetti,
picture by Gilbert Riswold

All Kinds of Neighbors

by Howard R. Wellesley,
pictures by Aliki

Some neighbors make **loud** noises.

Some do not.

113

Some neighbors play outdoors.

Some do not.

Some neighbors give PARTIES.

Some do not.

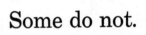

Some neighbors always *hurry*.

Some do not.

Some neighbors
ask you
to come in.

Some do not.

119

What kind of a neighbor are you?

Summer Morning

Bright and early,
Winds are waking,
Clouds are curly....

Everything
   is rosy, pearly,
Summer morning
   Bright and early.

by Barbara Young,
picture by Gilbert Riswold

Sally and Manda

are two little lizards
Who gobble up flies
in their two little gizzards.
They live by a toadstool
near two little hummocks
And crawl all around
on their two little stomachs.

by Alice B. Campbell,
picture by Robert M. Quackenbush

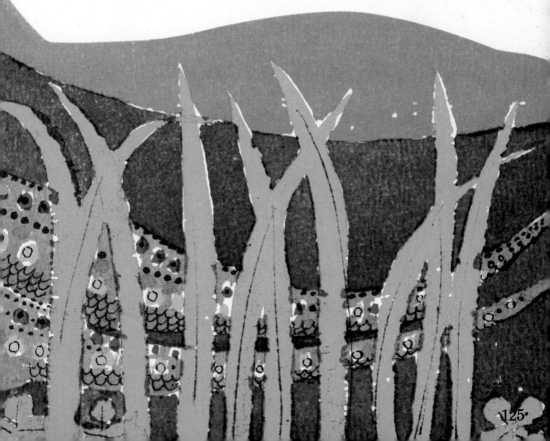

125

Here's a Picture for Dreaming

The Sun Is A Star

by Sune Engelbrektson,
pictures by Eric Carle

We see one star
in the daytime.
Do you know
its name?

The nighttime stars
   are very far away.
They look like
   tiny points of light.
If our sun
   were as far away
   as the other stars,
   it, too, would look like
   a tiny point of light.

Imagine that
   this flashlight
   is a distant star.
The flashlight
   looks bright
   in the darkness,
   doesn't it?

But, now,
    look at the light
    of the flashlight
    in the daytime.
The light cannot be seen
    from far away.
    Do you know why?

Our nearest star, the sun,
    is so bright
    that it keeps us
    from seeing the light
    of the flashlight
    in the daytime.
The sun's brightness
    also keeps us
    from seeing the light
    of other stars
    in the daytime.

Firefly by Elizabeth Madox Roberts, painting by Muriel Wood

A little light is going by,
Is going up to see the sky,
A little light with wings.

I never could have thought of it,
To have a little bug all lit
And made to go on wings.

THREE LITTLE MICE SAT DOWN TO SPIN. PUSSY PASSED BY AND SHE PEEPED IN. "WHAT ARE YOU DOING, MY LITTLE MEN?" "WE'RE WEAVING COATS FOR GENTLEMEN." "SHALL I COME IN AND SNIP OFF YOUR THREADS?" "NO, NO, MISS PUSSY, YOU'D BITE OFF OUR HEADS." "OH, NO, I'LL NOT, I'LL HELP YOU TO SPIN." "THAT MAY BE SO, BUT YOU DON'T COME IN."

an old rhyme, picture by Sal Murdocca, lettering by Ray Barber

137

Big Frogs, Little Frogs

by Patricia K. Miller and Iran L. Seligman,
pictures by Lee Ames

Big frogs.
Little frogs.
Leaping frogs.
Sleeping frogs.
Swimming frogs
.....and tadpoles.

Listen to the frogs!
Croak!
Croak!
Peep!
Gr-r-ump!

These are frog eggs.
They look like jelly.
Each black dot is
    the beginning of a tadpole.

Tadpoles are baby frogs.
Tadpoles are born from eggs.
They live like fishes in the water.

The tadpoles are growing.
Oh, how fast they grow.
They are turning into frogs.

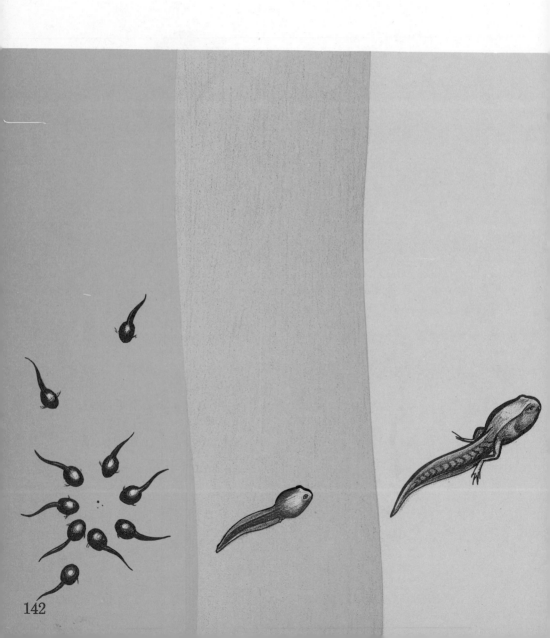

Tell me, little frog,
　　what happened to your tail?

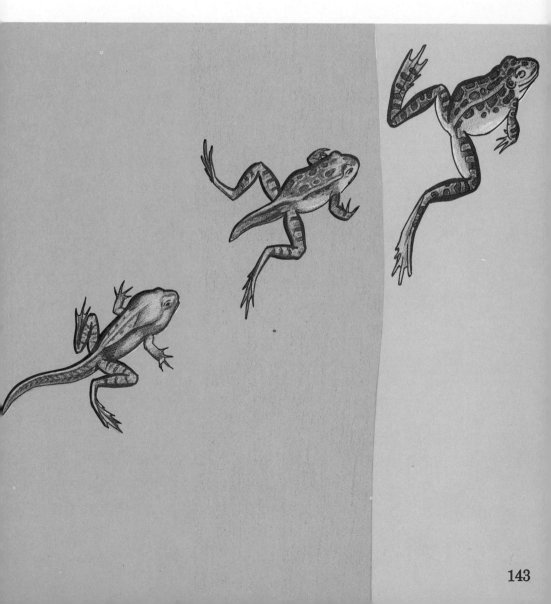

Big frogs.
Little frogs.

Leaping frogs.
Sleeping frogs.

Swimming frogs.

.....And tadpoles.

Listen to the frogs!

Croak!
Croak! Croak!

Peep! Peep! Peep! Peep!

GR-R-UMP!

Sun on the Clover

There's sun on the clover
And sun on the log,
Sun on the fish pond
And sun on the frog,

Sun on the honeybee,
Sun on the crows,
Sun on the wash line
To dry the clean clothes.

by Louise Fabrice Handcock,
picture by Gilbert Riswold

Here's a Picture for Storytelling

by Ed Renfro

From: *The People, Yes* by Carl Sandburg, picture by Henry Markowitz

The little girl saw her first troop parade and asked,
    "What are those?"
"Soldiers."
"What are soldiers?"
"They are for war. They fight and each tries to kill
    as many of the other side as he can."
The girl held still and studied.
"Do you know...I know something?"
"Yes, what is it you know?"
"Sometime they'll give a war
    and nobody will come."

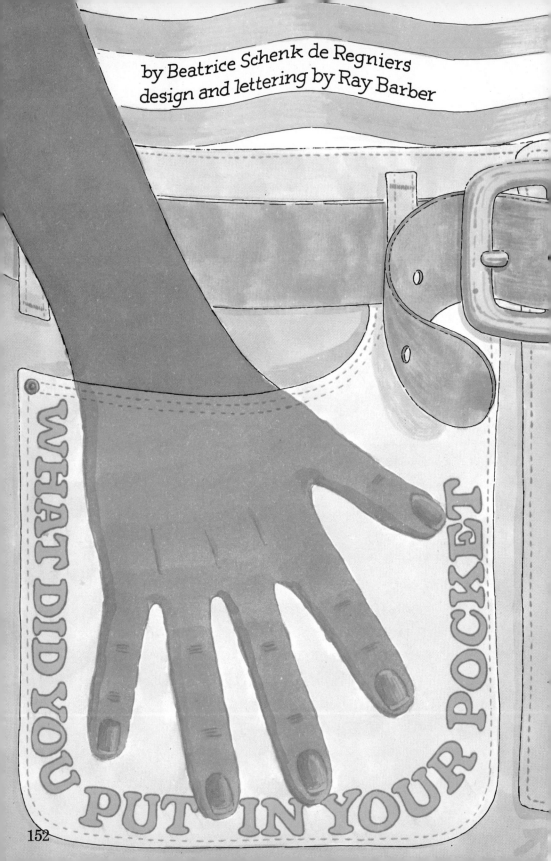

by Beatrice Schenk de Regniers
design and lettering by Ray Barber

WHAT DID YOU PUT IN YOUR POCKET

What did you put in your pocket
What did you put in your pocket
in your pockety pockety pocket
Early Monday morning?

I put in some chocolate pudding
I put in some chocolate pudding
slushy glushy pudding
Early Monday morning.

SLUSHY GLUSHY PUDDING

153

What did you put in your pocket
What did you put in your pocket
in your pockety pockety pocket
Early Tuesday morning?

I put in some ice-cold water
I put in some ice-cold water
nicy icy water
Early Tuesday morning.

SLUSHY GLUSHY
PUDDING
NICY ICY WATER

154

What did you put in your pocket
What did you put in your pocket
in your pockety pockety pocket
Early Wednesday morning?

I put in a scoop of ice cream
I put in a scoop of ice cream
slurpy glurpy ice cream
Early Wednesday morning.

SLUSHY GLUSHY
PUDDING
NICY ICY WATER
SLURPY GLURPY
ICE CREAM

155

What did you put in your pocket
What did you put in your pocket
in your pockety pockety pocket
Early Thursday morning?

I put in some mashed potatoes
I put in some mashed potatoes
fluppy gluppy potatoes
Early Thursday morning.

SLUSHY GLUSHY PUDDING
NICY ICY WATER
SLURPY GLURPY
ICE CREAM
FLUPPY GLUPPY
POTATOES

What did you put in your pocket
What did you put in your pocket
in your pockety pockety pocket
Early Friday morning?

I put in some sticky molasses
I put in some sticky molasses
sticky icky molasses
Early Friday morning.

SLUSHY GLUSHY PUDDING
NICY ICY WATER
SLURPY GLURPY ICE CREAM · FLUPPY
GLUPPY POTATOES
STICKY ICKY MOLASSES

What did you put in your pocket
What did you put in your pocket
in your pockety pockety pocket
Early Saturday morning?

I put in my five fingers
I put in my five fingers
funny finny fingers
Early Saturday morning.

SLUSHY GLUSHY PUDDING
NICY ICY WATER
SLURPY GLURPY ICE
CREAM FLUPPY
GLUPPY POTATOES
STICKY ICKY MOLASSES
FUNNY FINNY FINGERS

What did you put in your pocket
What did you put in your pocket
in your pockety pockety pocket
Early Sunday morning?

I put in a clean white handkerchief
I put in a clean white handkerchief
a spinky spanky handkerchief
Early Sunday morning.

SLUSHY GLUSHY PUDDING
NICY ICY WATER
SLURPY GLURPY ICE
CREAM FLUPPY
GLUPPY POTATOES
STICKY ICKY MOLASSES
FUNNY FINNY FINGERS

SPINKY SPANKY
HANDKERCHIEF

159

The House Biter

by William D. Sheldon,

pictures by Dan Dickas

I am
   a house biter.
I am
   a big, strong house biter.

I bite
  this little house
  because this little house
  is in the way.

The workmen
are going to build
a new house here.

I bite
  this big house
  because this big house
  is in the way.

The workmen
are going to build
a new road here.

I bite
  this gas station
  because this gas station
  is in the way.

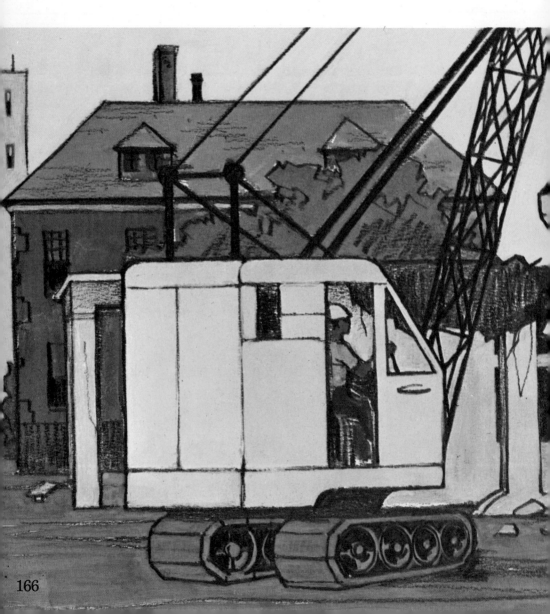

The workmen
are going to build
an apartment house here.

I bite
this school
because this school
is too old.

The workmen
are going to build
a new school here.

I bite and bite and bite……

I bite and bite and bite……

WHO IS TAPPING
AT MY WINDOW?

by A. G. Deming
design by Eric Carle

It's not I

said the cat.

It's not I

said the rat.

It's not I

said the wren.

It's not I

said the hen.

It's not I

said the fox.

It's not I

said the ox.

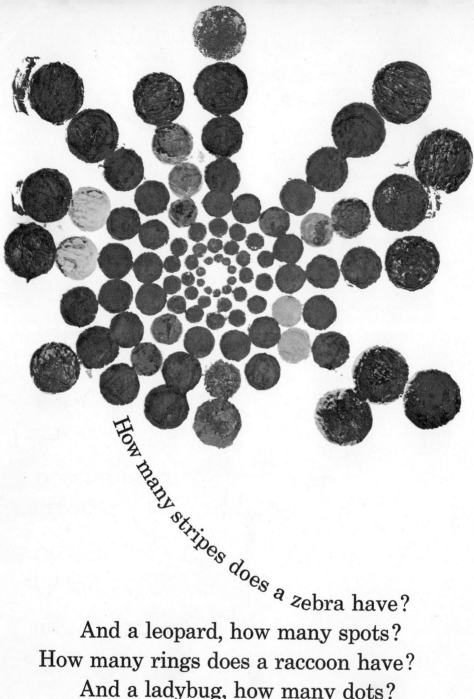

How many stripes does a zebra have?
And a leopard, how many spots?
How many rings does a raccoon have?
And a ladybug, how many dots?

poem by Philip Keils, artist unknown

a backward language story by H. R. Wright

Bat Is Whig?

Ty mame is nommy.
I am vot bery nig.

I am not as gig as a boat.
A boat is gigger than I am.

I am not as hig as a borse.
A borse is higger than I am.

I am not as ig as a phelebant.
A phelebant is igger than I am.

I am not as whig as a bale.
A bale is whigger than I am.

I am not as dig as a binosaur.
A binosaur is the diggest kning
     I thow.

The Mouse and The Flower

by Jay Ellis

There was a mouse
walking in summer.

He found an odd flower.

He
hugged it.

He jumped
into the blossom and stuck
his nose between all the
petals.

He stayed under it and
enjoyed it; it grew.

Insects and birds visited.

Friends picnicked under it.

Fall came; the flower died; it dropped five seeds. Mouse nestled them into the ground.

Winter came; Mouse slept beneath the seeds.

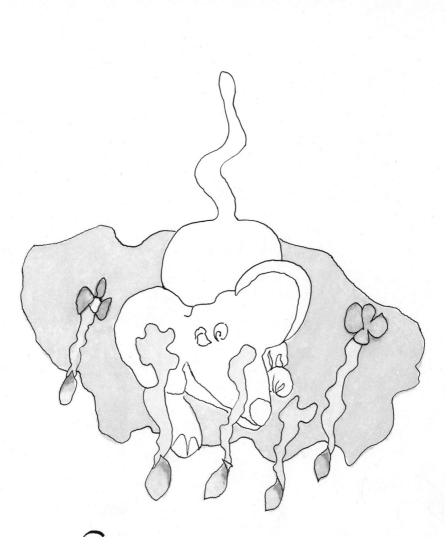

Spring came;
Mouse cared for
the seeds.

Summer came;
Mouse hugged
five new flowers.

painting by Seong Moy

The Sun Through My Window

Morning Comes Early

And bright with dew,
Under your window
I'll sing to you,
Up then with singing,
Up then with singing,
Let us be greeting
The morn so new.

Why do you linger
So long in bed?
Open the window
And show your head,
Up then with singing,
Up then with singing,
Over the meadow
The sun shines red. an old song

The Big Clock

Slowly ticks the big clock;

Tick-tock, Tick-tock!

But Cuckoo clock ticks double quick;

Tick-a-tock-a, tick-a-tock-a,
Tick-a-tock-a, tick!

author unknown,
picture by Kiyoaki Komoda

cuckoo!
cuckoo!